This journal belongs to

About

Intended Parent _____

Intended Parent _____

Other Children _____

Current City _____

Family background

The story so far

Why surrogacy?

The people that have supported this journey

How the search started

A little bit of help

Surrogate's name
Her family
She lives in
More about our surrogate

_____
_____
_____
_____
_____
_____
_____
_____
_____
_____
_____
_____

A little bit of help

Egg donor

Sperm donor

More about those that have chosen to help

_____
_____
_____
_____
_____
_____
_____
_____
_____
_____
_____
_____
_____
_____
_____

A little bit of help

Social Groups or support networks

A little bit of help

Friends and Family supporting the journey

Medical stuff

Agency or Independent ....
Location ....
Coordinator names ....
Doctors names ....

Medical Screening
When ....
Where ....
Results ....

Counselling
When ....
Where ....
Results ....

Contracts
Legal Rep ....
Where ....
Contracts signed on ....

Notes

Medical stuff

Notes

Medical stuff

Notes

___
___
___
___
___
___
___
___
___
___
___
___
___
___
___
___
___

Transfer Day

Date ....
Clinic ....
Who was there ....

The precious embryos

..........day old embryo/s

Quality ....

Number transferred ....

The two week wait

Thought and feelings during this time

....
....
....
....

1st +HPT   1st Beta   2nd Beta   Due Date

Ultrasounds

Date ....
Weeks ....
Results ....

Date ....
Weeks ....
Results ....

Ultrasounds

Date .... Date ....
Weeks .... Weeks ....
Results .... Results ....

Ultrasounds

Date ....
Weeks ....
Results ....

Date ....
Weeks ....
Results ....

Ultrasounds

Date ....   Date ....
Weeks ....   Weeks ....
Results ....   Results ....

Ultrasounds

Date ....
Weeks ....
Results ....

Date ....
Weeks ....
Results ....

Ultrasounds

Date .... Date ....
Weeks .... Weeks ....
Results .... Results ....

Appointments

Date ....
Weeks Pregnant ....
Stats ....
Results
....

Date ....
Weeks Pregnant ....
Stats ....
Results
....

Date ....
Weeks Pregnant ....
Stats ....
Results
....

Date ....
Weeks Pregnant ....
Stats ....
Results
....

Notes

Appointments

Date ....
Weeks Pregnant ....
Stats ....
Results
....

Date ....
Weeks Pregnant ....
Stats ....
Results
....

Date ....
Weeks Pregnant ....
Stats ....
Results
....

Date ....
Weeks Pregnant ....
Stats ....
Results
....

Date ....
Weeks Pregnant ....
Stats ....
Results
....

Date ....
Weeks Pregnant ....
Stats ....
Results
....

Appointments

Date ……………..
Weeks Pregnant ……….
Stats ………………………
Results
……

Date ……………..
Weeks Pregnant ……….
Stats ………………………
Results
……

Date ……………..
Weeks Pregnant ……….
Stats ………………………
Results
……

Date ……………..
Weeks Pregnant ……….
Stats ………………………
Results
……

Date ……………..
Weeks Pregnant ……….
Stats ………………………
Results
……

Date ……………..
Weeks Pregnant ……….
Stats ………………………
Results
……

Communication

Keep memories of conversations with your surrogate, pics and ultrasounds of your growing baby, or anything meaningful to you throughout the journey here

Communication

Communication

Communication

Communication

Journal

Date ....
Weeks Pregnant ....
Thoughts and feelings
....
....
....

Date ....
Weeks Pregnant ....
Thoughts and feelings
....
....
....

Date ....
Weeks Pregnant ....
Thoughts and feelings
....
....
....

Date ....
Weeks Pregnant ....
Thoughts and feelings
....
....
....

Date ....
Weeks Pregnant ....
Thoughts and feelings
....
....
....

Journal

Date ....
Weeks Pregnant ....
Thoughts and feelings
....
....
....

Date ....
Weeks Pregnant ....
Thoughts and feelings
....
....
....

Date ....
Weeks Pregnant ....
Thoughts and feelings
....
....
....

Date ....
Weeks Pregnant ....
Thoughts and feelings
....
....
....

Date ....
Weeks Pregnant ....
Thoughts and feelings
....
....
....

Journal

Date ....
Weeks Pregnant ....
Thoughts and feelings
....
....
....

Date ....
Weeks Pregnant ....
Thoughts and feelings
....
....
....

Date ....
Weeks Pregnant ....
Thoughts and feelings
....
....
....

Date ....
Weeks Pregnant ....
Thoughts and feelings
....
....
....

Date ....
Weeks Pregnant ....
Thoughts and feelings
....
....
....

Journal

Date ....
Weeks Pregnant ....
Thoughts and feelings
....
....
....

Date ....
Weeks Pregnant ....
Thoughts and feelings
....
....
....

Date ....
Weeks Pregnant ....
Thoughts and feelings
....
....
....

Date ....
Weeks Pregnant ....
Thoughts and feelings
....
....
....

Date ....
Weeks Pregnant ....
Thoughts and feelings
....
....
....

Journal

Date ....
Weeks Pregnant ....
Thoughts and feelings
....
....
....

Date ....
Weeks Pregnant ....
Thoughts and feelings
....
....
....

Date ....
Weeks Pregnant ....
Thoughts and feelings
....
....
....

Date ....
Weeks Pregnant ....
Thoughts and feelings
....
....
....

Date ....
Weeks Pregnant ....
Thoughts and feelings
....
....
....

Favorite Quotes & Inspirational words

Favorite Quotes & Inspirational words

Birth Day

How it began on the day

Who was there

Birth location

Medication received

Feelings

Baby Stats

Name/s ....

Date of Birth ....

Weight ....

Height ....

Baby Stats

Name/s ....

Date of Birth ....

Weight ....

Height ....

At the hospital

At the hospital

The Birth Story

The Birth Story

Our Family

Our Family

Our Family

Our Family

Our Family

Going Home

Going Home

Time with your surrogate

Time with your surrogate

Time with your surrogate

Our Family

Meeting the Family

Meeting the Family

Meeting the Family

Meeting the Family

Meeting the Family

Meeting the Family

The Nursery

The Nursery

Travel along the way

Travel along the way

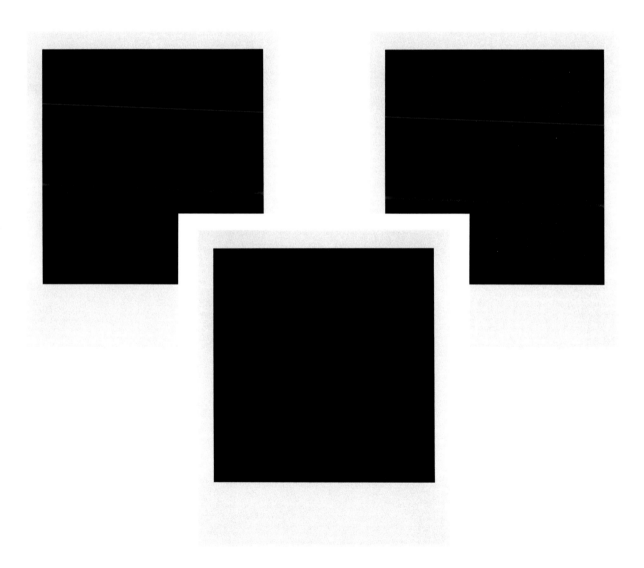

Travel along the way

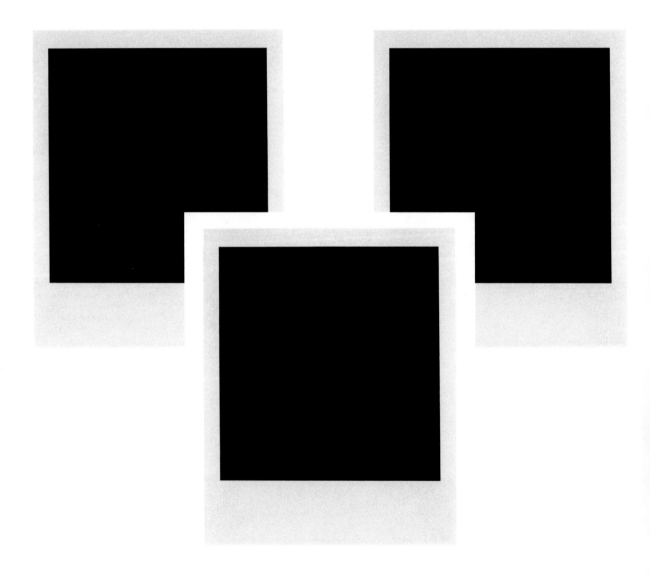

Memories & Keepsakes

Memories & Keepsakes

Memories & Keepsakes

Memories & Keepsakes

Memories & Keepsakes

Memories & Keepsakes

Memories & Keepsakes

Memories & Keepsakes

Made in the USA
Coppell, TX
19 November 2021